GARY LOCK, P
JOHN WILCOCI

COMPUTER ARCHAEOLOGY

SHIRE ARCHAEOLOGY

2

Cover photograph
A computer being used to display a drawing of a pot from an iron age site.
(Photograph: Peter Rogers.)

British Library Cataloguing in Publication Data available

Published by
SHIRE PUBLICATIONS LTD
Cromwell House, Church Street, Princes Risborough,
Aylesbury, Bucks HP17 9AJ, UK

Series Editor: James Dyer

ISBN 0 85263 877 9

First published 1987

Set in 11 point Times and printed in Great Britain by
C. I. Thomas & Sons (Haverfordwest) Ltd,
Press Buildings, Merlins Bridge, Haverfordwest, Dyfed.

Contents

Acknowledgements

The authors express their gratitude to Ruth Parker for assistance in the production of this book; also to Peter Rogers for the front cover photograph; to North Staffordshire Polytechnic Audio Visual Aids Unit; and to *Science and Archaeology* for permission to reproduce some diagrams.

John Wilcock would like to thank North Staffordshire Polytechnic for allowing research time and for making a small grant towards preparation costs.

List of illustrations

1
Introduction: computers in archaeology

Upon first consideration, a discipline such as archaeology might be thought to be incompatible with computing. The popular image of the archaeologist might well be of a leisurely digger in the Valley of the Kings, and this is clearly at odds with the computing image of prosaic grey boxes, keyboards and flashing lights. But practising archaeologists know that modern archaeology consists of hard physical work, often against the clock and in bad weather conditions, a rescue operation in advance of the bulldozers. Thus archaeology has had to move with the times and has borrowed techniques from most of the natural sciences. Examples are resistivity and magnetic surveying, radiocarbon dating, thermoluminescent dating, neutron activation analysis, pollen analysis, dendrochronology and microfauna, to mention but a few. Archaeologists should not be surprised, therefore, at the advent of the computer in archaeology; compared with other scientific techniques the computer is a tool of great power, for it is very flexible and has a wide variety of applications.

This book follows the basic division of computer applications in archaeology into two main areas. The first is the collection and storage of archaeological data. After introductory chapters discussing computer hardware, software and data structure, we will describe the different archaeological situations where computers are used as sophisticated filing systems. The following chapters look at the manipulation and presentation of archaeological data. These are mainly concerned with statistical techniques, the computer in this guise being a tool which applies statistical techniques to archaeological data. A glossary of technical terms appears at the end of this book, and inclusion of a word in the glossary is indicated in the text by italic type.

2
About computers

The world of computer technology is a complex and rapidly changing one. Fortunately, it is not necessary for archaeologists to enter very far into this world to be able to use a computer productively. It is desirable, however, for archaeologists to have a basic knowledge of the different parts of a computer and what they do. This will help the archaeologist to assess the potential of any particular machine or program. It will also help communication between specialists in the two very different disciplines of archaeology and computer science. This chapter provides such a grounding and is divided into two sections, *hardware* and *software*.

Hardware

Hardware refers to all the physical apparatus of a computer system, both electronic and mechanical. Any computer system consists of three parts:

1. The *central processing unit* (CPU) is the nerve centre of the computer. This controls all the other parts and performs the manipulation of the data as instructed by programs. Data and programs have to be loaded into the *memory* before they can be used.

2. For permanent storage of data and programs *backing store* is utilised; this is some form of *magnetic tape* or *disc*.

3. The user communicates with the CPU via *input/output (I/O) devices;* the usual ones are a keyboard and printer.

To store and process information a computer reduces it to binary form, that is a number system using only the two digits 0 and 1. Each binary digit is called a *bit,* eight bits are called a *byte* and one byte is needed to store one alphanumeric *character.* Computer storage capacities, therefore, are measured in terms of bytes; a *kilobyte* (Kb) equals approximately one thousand characters and a *megabyte* (Mb) approximately one million characters. Computers, especially microcomputers (micros), are also described according to the amount of information they process at one time. In the early 1980s most micros were 8 bit machines, and in the later 1980s they were 16 bit machines, with faster speeds and larger memories.

Mainframe computers are large, permanently fixed machines, usually situated within large establishments such as educational institutions, large firms or administrative offices. Because of their speed and power they can perform many different tasks at once, each task being controlled by a different user at a remote terminal. Mainframes have permanent teams of operators and programmers to service them and the average user probably never sees the actual machine.

Minicomputers are small versions of mainframes. They are permanently fixed and multi-user.

Microcomputers became increasingly commoner and less expensive during the 1970s with advances in silicon chip technology. A single chip performs all the functions of a CPU (a microprocessor), allowing the finished computer to be very compact and movable. Some very small micros are truly portable because they can be powered by batteries. Microcomputers are single-user machines.

Figure 1 shows a typical early 1980s machine with the CPU in the central box, a monitor (a television-like screen), a keyboard and a *floppy disc* about to be loaded into the *disc drive*. Such machines have become very common in archaeology because they are relatively inexpensive. As we shall see later, however, the large size and complex nature of archaeological data-sets can cause problems for the small memories and storage facilities of microcomputers.

There are two main storage media, magnetic tapes and magnetic discs, although discs are much commoner. A major disadvantage with tape is that it provides only *serial access;* the whole tape has to be read from the beginning to find the required piece of information. The main use of tape is to provide an archive copy of information kept on discs.

A magnetic disc provides *direct access* so that specific information stored on it can be reached immediately by the disc reading head. Discs can be rigid or floppy and fixed or exchangeable. Mainframes use packs of rigid discs with 200 Mb or more of storage whereas micros use exchangeable floppy discs with a capacity of typically 1 Mb each. Some microcomputer systems can also have fixed rigid discs added to them; these are usually referred to as *Winchester discs.*

The commonest type of input device for a microcomputer is a keyboard used in conjunction with a monitor screen. Mainframes use *visual display units* (VDUs), which consist of a keyboard and monitor combined into one device. Other input devices such as teletypes, card and tape readers became obsolete in the 1970s. A specialised graphics input device is a *digitising table* or *tablet.* This

1. Typical microcomputer with floppy disc backing store being used to display and process Anglo-Saxon pottery types. (Software: Julian Richards; photograph: North Staffordshire Polytechnic Audio Visual Aids Unit.)

records a line as a series of X and Y point coordinates via a movable stylus or crosswires which is positioned and then activated.

The standard form of output device which produces a permanent or *hard copy* is a *printer*. Mainframe computers use line printers, which print a whole line simultaneously. Microcomputers can be attached to a *dot matrix* printer, which produces each letter by a combination of dots, or to a daisy-wheel printer, which operates like a standard typewriter and prints a whole letter. The former type is usually less expensive and therefore commoner, although daisy-wheels produce a higher-quality print, which may be necessary for publications. Specialised VDUs can be used to produce high-resolution graphics while *plotters* produce graphical hard copy. Drum plotters are the expensive type in which a continuous roll of paper moves along one axis and the pen along the other axis. In flatbed plotters the sheet of paper is fixed and the pen moves in all directions. Some plotters will use several pens so that multicoloured drawings are possible.

Software

The term software simply means computer programs. A program is a set of coded instructions which tell the computer what to do; the detailed syntax of the code depends on the computer *language* being used.

All computers have an *operating system*. This is a set of programs supplied with the machine which controls the hardware and acts as an interface between the hardware and the user. Some operating systems are machine-specific, while others can be used on several different makes of machine. CP/M and MS-DOS were two common micro operating systems of the early 1980s and UNIX was designed for minicomputers and mainframes.

There is a whole group of programs known as assemblers, compilers and interpreters. These translate high-level languages to machine codes as used by the hardware.

It is a matter of personal choice whether to use your own written program or a commercially available *package*. Packages will adequately perform many of the tasks which are common in archaeology although other, more specific problems will warrant a specially written program. The pros and cons of either approach are many; packages, for example, are often expensive and may include refinements which are not necessary for the current job. Programming, on the other hand, can take years of work, time which could be spent on other things.

Most microcomputers come supplied with their own version of BASIC. Although this language is very easy to use it has serious disadvantages. It is not very portable between different machines because there are so many different versions of it. It is not a well structured language and so bad programming practice can easily evolve. BASIC is also slow, compared to other languages, when performing complex tasks because of the way the CPU interprets the instructions. Each mainframe machine usually has a much wider selection of languages available. These are all also available for the more powerful micros although, again, they can be expensive.

FORTRAN has been a popular language for many years. Because it is good for mathematical manipulations but rather poor at text handling it is traditionally used for more scientific applications. COBOL is the opposite in being a powerful text processor but mathematically weak and is therefore often used in commercial contexts such as for bank statements and pay slips. PASCAL is a structured language useful for both mathematical operations and text handling, but largely superseded by the language C, which may become a standard language in future. Some languages are designed for specific applications; PRO-LOG, for example, is used in artificial intelligence applications.

Commercially available packages can be categorised according to their function: a *database* management system (DBMS) is a suite of programs that collects, stores and retrieves data in an organised, automatic way. The internal workings of the system are complex but invisible to the user, who communicates through simple commands, often in the form of real language answers to questions. DBMSs are, therefore, usually *user-friendly*.

Common microcomputer DBMSs are dBaseII, dBaseIII and MDBS, which will run under several different operating systems. SIR and ORACLE are mainframe packages which will generally perform more complex tasks, in less time and on more data than their micro counterparts. This, however, is due to the hardware limitations of the smaller machines. Specialist DBMSs are also available; FAMULUS, for example is designed for text handling and is often used by historians and librarians.

A statistical package performs a range of analyses from simple descriptive statistics, such as mean and standard deviation (see chapter 5), to complex multivariate techniques (see chapter 6). These are not so common on microcomputers because of the processing power needed. SPSS-PC is a micro version of the popular mainframe package SPSS (Statistical Package for the Social Sciences). Specialist statistical packages also exist. CLUS-TAN is a mainframe package offering several different versions of a multivariate technique known as cluster analysis which is often used in archaeology.

A graphics package allows the user to make line drawings, either on the screen or as a hard copy, although special hardware is often needed as already described. The GSX graphics facility

runs under CP/M and is available for many micros. GINO-F and
PICASO are mainframe packages which will, again, usually
process much larger data files. SYMAP is a specialised graphics
package which has been used in archaeology for mapping and
spatial analyses.

Word-processing packages are probably the best known of all
computer packages. They allow the production and editing of text
and have many advantages over traditional typewriters. They are
not so common on mainframe computers and would be an
under-use of such powerful machines. Wordstar is the most
popular micro word processing package and runs under several
operating systems; others are machine-specific such as Wordwise
for the BBC microcomputer. Word-processing packages perform
just one function in a whole range of office management
functions for which packages are available, for example accounts
and order processing.

3
About data

Having looked briefly at the main features of hardware and software we must now say something about *data*.

The first thing to remember is that computerisation does not make the data more objective. A 'result' is always produced by the computer, but the meaning of the result, if any, should still be a product of human decision making. The problems that have arisen with the computerisation of archaeological data, therefore, are mainly due to the form of the data that archaeologists have chosen to record. There are two main problem areas; firstly archaeological data-sets tend to be very large and these often have to be processed on machines provided by budgets which are very small. Secondly, archaeological data are usually a mixture of different types of data. To investigate both of these areas further we need to look at the structure of data and introduce some definitions.

When data are stored on a computer they are organised in a hierarchical manner as shown in figure 2.

A *character* is the smallest unit of information available to the user and consists of one key depression on the keyboard which contains the full character set.

A *field* is the smallest unit of information relevant to the current computer process. When data held in fields are to be analysed they are then called variables. These two terms are, therefore, somewhat interchangeable.

A *record* is a collection of logically related fields. Each record usually consists of the same number of fields in the same order. In statistical analyses records are often called cases.

A *file* is a collection of logically related records. A collection of related files may be referred to as a databank or data-set.

This data structure can be illustrated with an example. The finds from an excavation may be recorded in separate files of information, with a pottery file, an animal bones file, a human bones file plus many others to make up the site databank. Each record within the pottery file will contain fields for pot type, fabric type, surface treatment, decoration, number and weight of sherds, amongst others. The other files will be structured differently to accommodate the required fields. Each field within a record will contain the appropriate number of characters needed to convey the information.

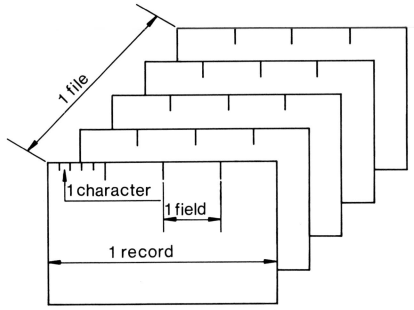

2. A schematic representation of the data hierarchy as used in computing, showing a character, a field, a record and a file.

Files vary according to how they can be accessed for reading from and writing to. The simplest type are *sequential* or serial files, in which records are processed one at a time, starting at the beginning. As already mentioned, magnetic tape allows only for serial files, whereas discs can contain these and other types.

An improvement on serial files is to organise the data by cross-indexing, as in *indexed sequential files*. A descriptive term (or field) is selected and the records are sorted according to the values which they have for this term, so that all records with the same term value occur together; thus a record with a specific value for this term is quickly found. The records sorted in this way form a major block and there is a major block sorted on each term. One part of the file may also be an index which serves to locate items in other parts of the file. As the name suggests, direct access files (sometimes called random access) can be accessed at any point. A common way of organising direct access files is by using a series of *keywords*. Thus to find all Roman bronze objects from layer 3 we need only look at the records for keywords ROMAN, BRONZE and LAYER 3 and determine which item numbers they have in common. Keywords are previously defined and may refer to any field: culture/period, material, provenance and types of artefact are frequent keywords.

It has already been stated that archaeological data usually consist of a mixture of different types. This is important because certain analyses can only be performed on data of a specific type, so how can data vary? There are two broad divisions of data: qualitative and quantitative, which result in four different levels of measurement.

Qualitative data — nominal (in name only). Such data have no numerical values initially, although values may be assigned by the archaeologist. 'Type of pottery' is a nominal variable which could have the values: 1 = jar, 2 = bowl and 3 = dish. The values 1, 2, and 3 are arbitrary and have no numeric value.

Quantitative data — ordinal (forming a sequence). These consist of a code (as nominal data) but have the property of ordering or ranking. An example is 'Site phase' where 1 = early, 2 = middle and 3 =late has an obvious order.

Quantitative data — interval (sequence with fixed distances). These data are ordered but with intervals of a fixed length; an example is the date in years. The distance between 350 BC and 50 BC is the same as between AD 100 and AD 400, although the numerical values are arbitrary and thus cannot be compared except to say that they are earlier or later.

Quantitative data — ratio (fixed distances with datum point). These have the properties of interval data but with a fixed, meaningful zero. An example is age. A site two thousand years old is twice as old as one one thousand years old.

Date is not a ratio type because 2000 BC is not twice as old as 1000 BC. These levels of measurement are especially important in the application of statistical tests, since some tests can only be applied to data of a specific type.

It is a common misconception that the computer requires data to be in some form of code, that is, expressed in combinations of letters and figures, or abbreviated in some way. This is incorrect: data may be in natural language, subject only to practical limitations on storage. Archaeologists are usually quick to insist that any computer system used by them must allow natural language data. Faced with the prospect of typing their information into the computer, however, they happily invent numerous abbreviations and codes.

The adoption of a rigorous *coding system* is good practice. It not only saves storage space but allows meaningful comparisons between data to be performed. Coding systems apply to qualitative variables, making them much more subjective than quantitative variables, which are objectively measured.

A nominal variable will consist of several categories which are represented by a code; an example might be 'name of county' in a file of archaeological sites. For the first three records the values could be: SOMERSET, DEVON, CORNWALL. This is a full keyword coding system, which is very wasteful of storage space because each county will be stored many times. An abbreviated keyword system may use the first four characters, thus: SOME, DEVO, CORN. This saves space but is rather cryptic. A more extreme version still would be a numeric code where each category has a unique number: 3, 12, 5. This is meaningless unless a code book is available for interpretation. It is possible for the computer to perform the interpretation invisibly so that the digit 3 is stored but the word SOMERSET is output.

Some data can be coded hierarchically, for example the pottery from the excavations at Danebury iron age hillfort (see Lock, 1984). Each sherd can be recorded down to four levels, thus J B 2 .1, where the characters represent pottery class (J), type (B), form (2) and variety (.1); this example is a shouldered jar with an everted rim and height less than or equal to the maximum diameter. A poor sherd may yield enough information for only the class to be established, in which case only J would be recorded. The Danebury classification scheme has four categories of class, thirteen types, 33 forms and 49 varieties. These data are not only recorded at different levels of the hierarchy but also may be analysed in this hierarchy. A simple pottery analysis may use only the class and type levels, whereas a very detailed breakdown would utilise all four levels.

Many archaeological data take the form of written descriptions which cannot be codified and which are, therefore, stored on the computer as free text. Because it is difficult to utilise free text for any form of analysis, it is usually confined to a 'comments' field at the end of each record, if it is included at all.

4
Different archaeological situations

We can now move on to look at five specific archaeological situations in which computers are used: in pre-excavation surveying, on excavations, in museums, in recording the heritage and in a miscellaneous group of specialist applications.

Pre-excavation surveys

It is common practice for archaeologists to perform a contour survey and a geophysical survey of a site to provide valuable information which can help excavation. These surveys are based on the site grid with readings taken at set intervals of usually 1 metre. The product, therefore, is a two-dimensional grid of data with each reading representing a third dimension, or a height. Computers are good at processing grids of readings and, as the data-sets from surveys tend to be large (a 100 metre square produces ten thousand readings), it is not surprising that they have been applied to this problem.

The results of these surveys have traditionally been presented in a graphical form. Two-dimensional contour maps are common and, in the case of geophysical surveys, dot-density maps (for example figure 3) are often used which show anomalous areas as darker shades. However, the power of modern hardware and software can produce much more exciting pictures which use the three-dimensional qualities of the data.

Wire-frame diagrams represent the data as a surface which can be viewed from any direction and at any height, and the vertical distances (the survey readings) can be exaggerated to bring out subtle features. Figure 4 shows the results of a resistivity survey of a Roman camp, while figure 5 shows a contour survey presented as a stereoscopic pair. This software (Spicer, 1985) will also produce red and green stereoscopic pictures which, when viewed through the appropriate spectacles, enhance the three-dimensional effect dramatically.

Excavations

Central to this and the next two applications are the *data-processing* tasks of *data capture* and *information retrieval*. As there is very little standardisation in archaeological computing these are performed by a variety of self-written programs and commercial database packages.

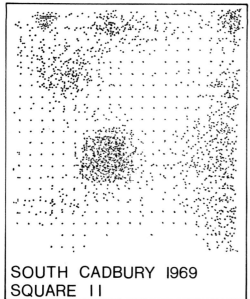

3. Typical square from a proton gradiometer survey, showing a pit as a large anomaly to the lower left of centre. Readings have been filtered by computer processing and output on a graph plotter. The density of the dot scatter is a function of the filtered reading strength. (Software: John Wilcock; copyright: *Science and Archaeology*; Site Director of South Cadbury excavations: Leslie Alcock.)

SOUTH CADBURY 1969
SQUARE II

Data capture on microcomputers is usually interactive via the keyboard and screen, but there are two main screen designs in common use: the form layout, and the question/answer technique. In the form layout method the computer displays one of several form layouts on the screen. Each consists of a number of data category headings with blanks for the insertion of free-format text. A flashing *cursor* indicates to the operator where the next piece of information is to be inserted. The text may be edited using special keys; for example, if a spelling mistake has been made the operator repositions the cursor over any one of the available character positions using keys for 'down one line', and 'up one line', 'forward one space', 'back one space' and 'beginning of page', then deletes or alters characters as appropriate. When the operator is satisfied with the text a control key is pressed which repositions the cursor to the beginning of the next piece of text (headings are protected and cannot be deleted or corrupted). When the whole page has been satisfactorily completed, the depression of a transmission key causes the whole record to be written to backing memory and simultaneously a hard copy of the record may be produced by the printer.

The second method consists of a string of questions which appear on the screen in sequence to be answered. Which questions are asked depends on previous answers, since the data structure is hierarchical, and some data categories may not exist for some artefacts; for example, if a pot has no handle, then no

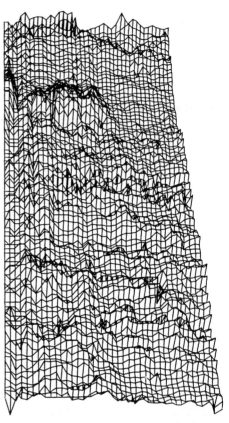

4. A wire-frame diagram representing the results of a resistivity survey at Stramshall, Staffordshire. Linear features (ditches) run into the area from the right-hand side. (Software: Dick Spicer, 1985; data: Gary Lock and Paul Reilly, 1985.)

questions need to be asked about the handle form, construction or decoration.

The whole aim of capturing and storing data is so that they can be retrieved in a meaningful way. Retrieval requests are specified in the form of keywords which can be joined by logical operators such as AND, OR and NOT. In this way complex requests can be built up like 'all stone circles within one kilometre of a water supply which have been excavated within the last ten years'. Each record found to satisfy the request can be output either in total or as specified fields of the record.

The feasibility of using a computer to store large amounts of archaeological information was demonstrated by the mid 1960s (Chenhall, 1967b) and databanks developed considerably in the late 1960s and early 1970s (Wilcock, 1969; Cowgill, 1973), chiefly in the United States, France and Britain. By the late 1970s a growing number of microcomputer installations was being moved around to excavations for on-site data capture (Graham, 1976;

Wilcock, 1978), and this continued in the early 1980s (Powlesland, 1983; Booth, Brough and Pryor, 1984). Formal encouragement for the use of the computer by British archaeologists was given by both the Frere Report and the Cunliffe Report. The first of these working parties, set up by the Ancient Monuments Board for England Committee for Rescue Archaeology, highlighted the crisis in publication of archaeological excavations caused by larger and more numerous sites, more extensive scientific and specialist studies and greatly increased printing costs. It proposed several distinct levels of publication:

Level I (museum storage): the site itself, general notes, old letters, previous accounts; excavated finds.

Level II (museum, regional or national archive): site notebooks, recording forms, drawings, audiotapes; artefact records, X-rays, photographs, negatives, colour transparencies.

Level III (articles or occasional papers, xerography, microfiche, computer printouts): full illustration and description of all structural and stratigraphical relationships, classified finds lists and drawings; specialist analyses.

5. A stereo-pair of wire-frame diagrams showing details of a contour survey of an early Christian burial ground on the Isle of Man. For stereo viewing hold a mirror on the centre line facing towards the right-hand side. (Software: Dick Spicer, 1985; data: Paul Reilly.)

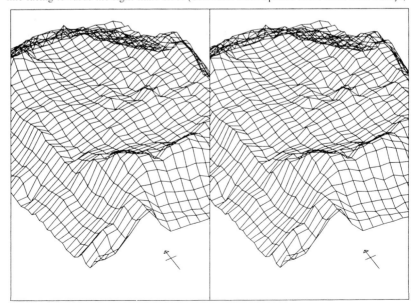

Level IV (the 'glossy' publication): synthesised descriptions; selected finds and specialist reports relevant to synthesis.

The place of the computer was at Level III. The second of the working parties, set up by the Council for British Archaeology and the Department of the Environment, heavily recommended computer processing of site data.

Most computerisation of excavation data is performed after the excavation; machines are not common in trenches! Data are usually recorded on site on a pro-forma sheet and then transferred on to the computer at a later date. The excavations at Danebury hillfort are an example of such a procedure where seventeen seasons have produced 15 Mb of data, and not all available information has been computerised.

Probably the best example of on-site data recording, however, is the work of Powlesland (1985) in Yorkshire. Here data are recorded on small hand-held micros and then transferred to a larger machine. Because the storage of these small machines is limited, the data have to be strictly codified and operators have to carry a code book. Despite these restrictions the system works and has been in use for many years.

One area of excavation where computers have considerable potential is the drawing of archaeological sections. In 1977 Duncan and Main illustrated a system which would produce publication-ready labelled or stippled sections (figure 6) although little has been done in 'real-life' situations.

Museums

Computerised museum catalogues developed in several countries, notably the United States (Chenhall, 1967a), France and Britain (Stewart, 1980; Light and Roberts, 1984).

From the middle 1960s the major effort in museum information retrieval in Britain was undertaken by members of the Information Retrieval Group of the Museums Association (IRGMA), which was renamed the Museums Documentation Association (MDA) in 1977. The draft proposals for an interdisciplinary museum cataloguing system were published by IRGMA in 1969.

By the early 1970s pilot studies had been carried out in several museum disciplines, and it was known that preparation of data for computer input added only about one twentieth of the cost to the existing cost of traditional cataloguing. Nevertheless, IRGMA decided in 1971 that a national computer archive on a single central machine, with records from all museums in the United Kingdom, was unrealistic. Systems designed to meet local

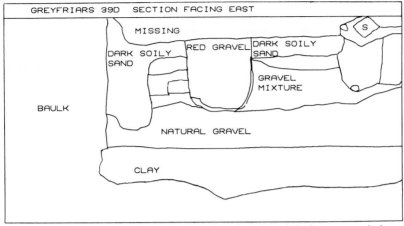

6. A computer-drawn section from an excavation. A variety of shading patterns is drawn by software and may be selected by user-machine interaction, for example (a) shows labelling and (b) stippling. (Software: Michael Duncan and Peter Main; copyright: *Science and Archaeology.*)

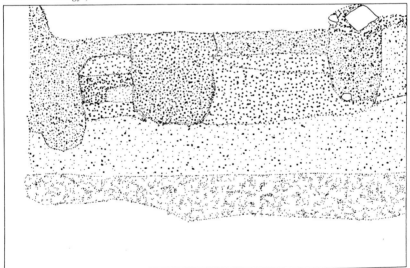

requirements, implemented on local computers, were felt to be more efficient.

Having decided to decentralise, therefore, IRGMA was forced to propose communication between individual local computer records by some hardware-independent means. Thus the 'high-level communication format' proposed by IRGMA in 1969 was born. This consisted of a defined series of categories of information. Ensuring direct communication between many local, incompatible computers would require the writing of an unacceptably high number of programs, for each of the computers would have to communicate with every other one; the idea was that, using the high-level communication format as an intermediary, only two programs would be required for each computer, to translate to and from the high-level format.

Thus we can see the IRGMA achievement in its true light, as a high-level communication format which defined the information structures, but which was independent of any particular computer hardware.

The data structure is hierarchical, employing several levels of sub-items, each type of data corresponding to a specific box on a custom-designed index card. Several such cards have been printed for use in museums, for fine art, geological specimens, history artefacts, mineralogical specimens, natural history specimens, scientific instruments, uniforms, bones and general 'museum objects', as well as for archaeology. They were designed by teams of museum curators, experts in the specific disciplines and information scientists to meet museum cataloguing requirements. All were subjected to a lengthy period of field trials, followed by assessment and redesign where necessary, and proved satisfactory in both manual and computerised reference systems.

The archaeology card was intended primarily for museum use, but it was hoped that field archaeologists would also use it, in the interests of compatibility and communication. This has indeed proved possible, although unusual; for example York Archaeological Trust began to use adaptations of the IRGMA cards in 1975.

The position by 1986 was typical of all aspects of computing in archaeology, showing a distinct lack of standardisation. Whilst many museums used the MDA system, others used incompatible computerised systems, and many others were not computerised at all. The MDA has a valuable advice service for any museum contemplating the use of a computer.

Recording the heritage

Archaeological sites of all periods and types are recorded in the county-based Sites and Monuments Record (SMR) or the country-based National Archaeological Record (NAR), which is part of the National Monument Record (NMR). Both these are being computerised.

By 1976 most areas of Britain had intensive record schemes, although relatively few were computerised. The NAR of the Royal Commission on Ancient and Historical Monuments (RCHM) were intensive, fully researched documents relating to particular sites or areas, as well as manuscripts, plans, maps, photographs, air photographs and ephemeral archaeological publications. Many of these were held on microfilm. The NAR for Wales in addition had a non-intensive set of record cards for sites, while the other areas of Britain relied on copies of the 300,000 Ordnance Survey archaeological cards originally produced for the entry of archaeological sites on published maps. Cambridge University Committee for Aerial Photography maintained an archive of many thousands of aerial photographs of archaeological sites. With regard to county records, the Northern Archaeological Survey had non-intensive computer records covering Northumberland, Durham, Tyne and Wear, and Cumbria. The County Archaeologists of most other English counties relied on duplicates of the Ordnance Survey cards, maps and registers organised by parish.

Laflin (1973) designed a fairly simple information retrieval system, and by 1976 it was in use by local archaeological groups for county records in Shropshire, Herefordshire, Worcestershire, Hertfordshire and Wiltshire on an experimental basis. Some other counties had records based on the IRGMA format (for example Merseyside), some a system developed by Benson at the Oxford City and County Museum (Warwickshire, Northamptonshire, Cambridgeshire, Berkshire and West Sussex, as well as Oxfordshire itself), while yet others independently followed the 1975 computer recommendations of the CBA Working Party on Archaeological Records (for example Staffordshire).

In Scotland there were no county-organised records, but in addition to the Royal Commission on Historical Monuments (Scotland) records there were card systems held in 1976 by planning officers, universities, museums and archaeological societies at Renfrew, East Lothian, Dunbartonshire, Cowal, St Andrews, Dundee, Aberdeen, Caithness and Shetland. In Wales the four county-based archaeological trusts have taken over responsibility of SMRs.

The number of SMRs which were computerised grew from only one out of a total of seventeen in 1974 to 34 out of 54 in 1984. Some of this was due to financial incentives from the Historic Buildings and Monuments Commission (now known as English Heritage). This body has also produced its own software (called

SAMSON and based on the SUPERFILE package), which SMRs are encouraged to use. Whether this will achieve standardisation remains to be seen.

The main output from these SMRs is in the form of catalogues in response to specific requests. Over a sample period of three and a half years the Dyfed Trust produced 350 catalogues, 35 per cent classified by period, 25 per cent by area, 15 per cent by site type and the rest unclassified.

The NMR for England has upgraded its system to a mainframe machine running the ORACLE DBMS, based at the RCHM's Southampton office.

Specialist applications

These are data-sets on well-defined themes maintained by specialists in various fields.

Many archaeologists keep private card-indexes of their work, and some of these have been inserted into computer files, but few have yet been made public. The reason for this could be that each acknowledged authority on a specific archaeological specialism is reluctant to surrender the basis of that authority, the information which has been absorbed and recorded over the years. Information means power, and it is in an acknowledged expert's own interests to be the only person to have hands on all of it. However, here are some examples of record structures which have been computerised: Roman inscriptions (Wilcock, 1981b); stone tools (Callow, 1976); bell beakers (Shennan and Wilcock, 1975); Roman pottery (Young, 1980); petroglyphs (Walker, 1981); medieval pottery (Wilcock, 1983); tree-ring measurements (Baillie, 1982); radiocarbon dates (Wilcock, Otlet and Walker, 1983).

It is these specialist files of information, often based on mainframe computers, which are often used for statistical analyses of various kinds. This leads us into the second major area of computer applications in archaeology.

5
Descriptive statistics and graphics

Computers are often used as tools to aid the application of statistical techniques. While it is true that many of these techniques have flourished because of computers, most of them have developed independently. This chapter and the next reflect the two functions of statistics: *descriptive statistics*, which present the data in a condensed form, and *inferential statistics*, which allow an archaeological theory to be tested.

Descriptive statistics are a set of techniques that aim to display the main features of a data-set quickly and easily. These features will very probably not be apparent in the numerical raw data, simply because of the sheer quantity of readings. Descriptive statistics, therefore, are methods of condensing large data-sets so that we can make sense of them. This is often done by using some form of pictorial (or graphical) display; the particular type of display will depend on the quality and type of data. Whichever one is used, it must be simple enough to show patterns within the data, such as trends and peaks, whilst containing sufficient detail, scales for example, to allow for proper interpretation. Many of these diagrams are two-dimensional in that they have two axes, each of which represents an archaeological variable.

Various kinds of diagram allow data to be plotted in different ways, and some statistical packages will produce these automatically. Figure 7 shows a cumulative frequency graph which has percentage as the vertical axis and pot-rim diameters along the horizontal axis. The lines represent different archaeological contexts and show the variation in pot sizes between them.

The lenticular diagram is another variation on the two axis theme which is particularly applicable in archaeology. Figure 8 shows one such diagram which again has percentage on the vertical axis but this time the horizontal axis represents time. An assemblage with four different types of artefact is broken down into relative proportions and plotted between the axes. This immediately shows the changing composition of the assemblage through time. Assuming time progresses towards the right-hand side, we can see that Type 2 is an early type while Type 4 is late and although Types 1 and 3 are both intermediate they have very different distributions.

If the data to be displayed are paired, and at least ordinal, a scatterplot will reveal any association. Figure 9 shows a scatter-

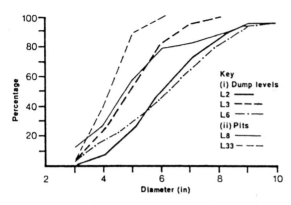

7. A cumulative percentage graph showing the relative occurrences of rim diameters for one functional pot type in different deposits of wasters at a Romano-British kiln site in Highgate Wood, London. (Data compiled by Clive Orton.)

plot for various types of pottery plotting their height by their rim diameter/height ratio. As might be expected, the jugs can be seen to be tall and narrow while plates are low and wide.

If there are three properties to be displayed, we can use the three-pole plot or triangular graph, as shown in figure 10. Each point (often an artefact) is positioned according to its values on the three axes. These diagrams can be useful for classification studies, as groups of points often emerge.

The commonest of all display techniques used in archaeology is the histogram. This is used to show the distribution of a variable which is measured on an interval or ratio scale. Examples of this type of variable met in archaeology are dimensions and weights of objects, volumes of pots, areas of habitation sites, and ratios of

8. A lenticular diagram to show the relative importance of artefact types with time. Artefacts 1 and 3 reach their maximum popularity during the time scale, 3 rising from 40 to 55 per cent then declining to 30 per cent while 1 grows from 0 to 45 per cent then declines to 0 per cent. Artefact 2 dies out from 60 to 0 per cent, while artefact 4 is introduced and grows from 0 to 70 per cent. Site assemblages A, B and C will, therefore, show different proportions of the artefact types. (Copyright: *Science and Archaeology.*)

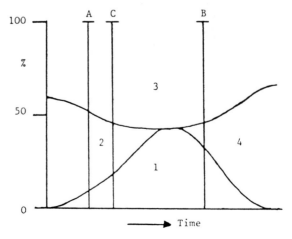

9. A scatterplot for a pair of attributes: height and rim diameter/height ratio for various generic 'types' of pot. Each artefact is shown as a dot or symbol, positioned by the values of the two attributes. Relations between artefacts are shown by their relative positions on the scatterplot (note the vagueness and overlap of these generic terms, particularly 'dish' and 'bowl'). Clusterings of dots may reveal significant groups of artefacts. (Copyright: *Science and Archaeology*; data compiled by Ann Hardy-Smith Andrews.)

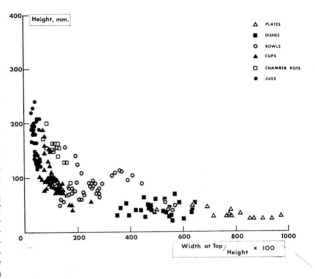

various measurements, for example maximum radius/height of a pot. The total relevant range of the variable is split into a number of intervals, and counts are made of the number of times the attribute values fall into each interval. The width of the interval used is important as different widths can make the same data appear very different. It is always a good idea to experiment with a variety of interval widths before coming to any conclusions. What is being measured is the area within the blocks so a scaled vertical axis (which measures the height of the blocks) can only be used if all the interval widths are equal as shown in figure 11. It is

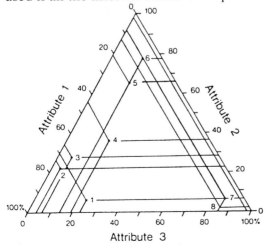

10. A three pole plot for three attributes. Each artefact is shown as a dot, for example artefact 3 has values attribute 1: 66 per cent attribute 2: 28 per cent attribute 3: 6 per cent.

11. A histogram for an assemblage of stilts (kiln furniture) by length. Four clear groups of stilts emerge, corresponding to four different sizes of pots fired in the kiln. (Software: John Wilcock; Site Director of Potters Fields, 1965: Francis Celoria.)

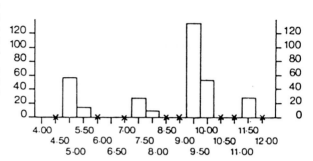

POTTERS FIELDS 1965

usually hoped that the histogram will show one or more peaks which can be interpreted in an archaeological way; figure 11 shows four such peaks. Figure 12 shows a typical application of a histogram in displaying the distribution of one species of pollen, which can be seen to change with time. Some graphics packages will produce three-dimensional histograms which can be viewed from any position. Figure 13 shows the results of a resistivity survey presented as a three-dimensional histogram. The horizontal axes are the site coordinates while each reading is shown as a vertical scaled column.

Bar charts are similar to histograms but they represent discrete rather than continuous variables. This means that the intervals along the horizontal axes are decided by the categories of the nominal variable being used. There is, however, usually no set

12. A pollen diagram showing relative pollen counts of one species at various sampling depths in a peat bog. The vertical axis expresses the pollen counts as percentages of the total count for all samples. The horizontal axis is depth in centimetres below the surface and can be taken as a measure of age. (Software: John Wilcock; copyright: *Science and Archaeology*.)

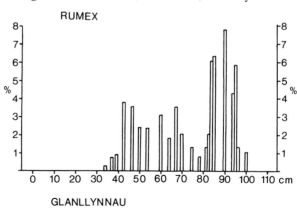

RUMEX

GLANLLYNNAU

Late Glacial

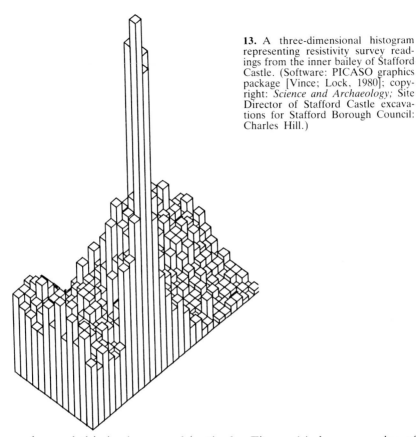

13. A three-dimensional histogram representing resistivity survey readings from the inner bailey of Stafford Castle. (Software: PICASO graphics package [Vince; Lock, 1980]; copyright: *Science and Archaeology;* Site Director of Stafford Castle excavations for Stafford Borough Council: Charles Hill.)

order and this is chosen subjectively. Figure 14 shows a series of bar charts representing relative proportions of different pottery types. In bar charts the blocks are always measured by their height and, again, peaks could suggest an archaeological significance.

A type of display which is quite popular in archaeology and gets away from the normal two axis theme is the piechart. The relative sizes of defined categories of the variable are shown as 'slices of the pie', the total being represented by the area of the circle. Figure 15 shows a piechart for the same data as figure 11.

Often in archaeology data have a spatial component and need to be displayed in an appropriate way. Distribution maps are the usual way of doing this and these can be generated by computer. Figure 16 shows a distribution map of various Roman sites in Britain. Care must be taken in interpreting such a map because it shows only the present state of knowledge, which is moulded by

POTTERY TYPES

1 2 3 4 5 6 7 8 9 10 11 12 13 14

Latest

Cultural
Levels
or
Contexts

Earliest

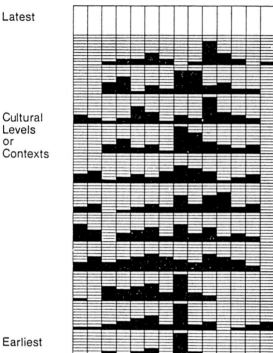

14. Bar charts showing the relative occurrences of defined pottery types in a succession of contexts (cultural phases). The pottery types are qualitative data and their order is arbitrary.

such factors as the distribution of excavations and of archaeologists active in the field. Distribution maps concerned with individual sites are also of interest to archaeologists. Figure 17 shows quantities of pottery found in all the early phase pits from the first ten years of excavation at Danebury hillfort.

It is usually of value to have summary statistics accompanying these pictorial displays. One of the commonest ways of doing this is to use an average, or more formally a measure of central tendency, of which there are three important ones. The median of a distribution is that value of the variable such that half of the values are less than it and half are more. It can be used on data that is at least ordinal, whereas the mean can only be used on interval or ratio data. The mean is the most popular measure and is found by dividing the total of the observations by the number of observations. The mode is that value of the variable which occurs the most frequently (shown by the peak in a histogram) and can be found for variables at any level of measurement. Figure 18 shows the distribution of pottery weights from a series of archaeological contexts. It can be seen that the mode, median and mean are different. This implies that the distribution is not symmetrical and is being distorted by a few high readings.

It is not enough, however, just to use a pictorial display and a measure of central tendency to describe the distribution of a variable; a numerical measure of variability or dispersion is also needed. These statistics describe the 'spread' of the values of a variable. The range of a set of observations is simply the difference between the smallest and largest. The quartiles (Q1, Q2 and Q3) are the three values that divide a distribution into four equal parts (so that Q2 is the median). These can be calculated from a cumulative frequency graph. The quartile deviation is found by subtracting Q1 from Q3 and dividing by 2. The most important and commonest measure of variability is the standard deviation. This is complicated to work out by hand but, along with all the other statistics mentioned above, is standard to all statistical packages.

Some data-sets present problems which are specific to archaeology and where standard descriptive methods such as those just described are not applicable. One such area is context

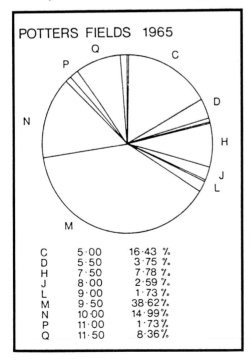

POTTERS FIELDS 1965

C	5·00	16·43 %
D	5·50	3·75 %
H	7·50	7·78 %
J	8·00	2·59 %
L	9·00	1·73 %
M	9·50	38·62%
N	10·00	14·99%
P	11·00	1·73%
Q	11·50	8·36%

15. Piechart for an assemblage of stilts (kiln furniture) by length, the same data as for figure 11. The largest group M has central value 9.50 cm and range 9.25 cm to 9.75 cm, forming over 38 per cent of the sample. Referring to the histogram of figure 11, the four modes are represented by slices C + D, H + J, M + N and Q. (Software: John Wilcock; Site Director of Potters Fields 1965: Francis Celoria.)

16. Distribution map for Roman Britain. (Software: John Wilcock; data compiled by Ordnance Survey.)

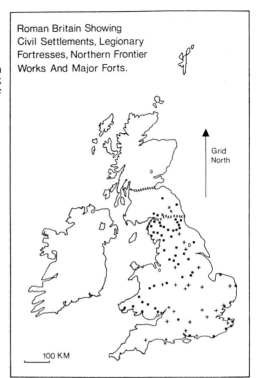

Roman Britain Showing Civil Settlements, Legionary Fortresses, Northern Frontier Works And Major Forts.

Grid North

100 KM

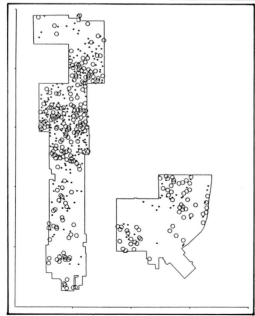

17. The first ten years of excavation at Danebury hillfort, Hampshire, showing all pits of the early phase. Small circles are pits containing less than the median value of sherds, large circles are pits with more than the median value. (Software: Gary Lock; data: Barry Cunliffe.)

sorting to produce Harris matrices. This is the standard archaeological procedure of sorting out the 'above', 'below' and 'same as' relationships between contexts found in an excavation to produce a linked matrix which forms the basis of the site's phasing. On a major urban excavation there may be tens of thousands of different contexts, and the working out of the phase diagram becomes an extremely complex and time-consuming task. The situation becomes aggravated in a rescue environment, where the drawing of the context relationship may be removed by several weeks or months from the excavation. Analysis of the context linkages then frequently reveals illogicalities in the data which must be resolved; relationships may have been recorded several times; and the same context may have given different numbers by excavation teams in different areas of the site. It is possible to use the computer to generate the Harris matrix so that duplicate relationships are detected quickly, dual numbering resolved and illogicalities indicated. The computer can produce in minutes a phase diagram that would take an archaeologist months to resolve by hand. The preparation of data for the STRATA computer program and its implementation on a microcomputer was described by Wilcock (1975, 1981a).

18. A histogram showing the distribution of weight of an artefact with its mode, median and mean. Notice how these three values are separated by the asymmetrical nature of the distribution due to a few large data values. (Source: Mike Fletcher.)

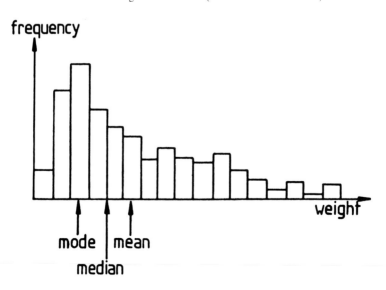

6
More complex statistics

Until about 1975 the vast majority of computer applications in archaeology were of a complex statistical nature carried out on a mainframe. This has gradually changed because microcomputers have become much more common and many archaeologists have access to one. Archaeologists are now trying to solve their own problems, which cover a wide range of applications as we have already seen. Much of the earlier work was carried out by statisticians with an interest in archaeology, probably attracted by the complexity of archaeological data-sets.

A large body of general statistical techniques which can be applied in a variety of circumstances has been developed since the early part of the twentieth century. They were not specifically designed for archaeological use, although some have been adapted slightly to fit specific archaeological problems. These are often referred to as inferential statistics because an archaeological hypothesis is tested by their use. Some of these tests involve the concept of probability, which determines how likely the result is compared to its chances of happening randomly. This chapter is divided into two parts; the first deals with bivariate statistical techniques, which test the relationship between two variables, while the second presents some multivariate statistical techniques, which use many variables. Multivariate techniques blur the boundary between descriptive and inferential statistics because one of their purposes is to condense large data-sets, often into a graphical form. Also their 'inferential' part may not be associated with a probability, so whether the result is 'correct' or not must be decided by the user.

To make some kind of sense of a data-set the archaeologist searches for patterns within it which are then translated into archaeological statements. The commonest patterns to be isolated are trends of variables through time or over an area, producing temporal or spatial distributions. 'Does the quantity of Type A pottery change through time?' or 'Which areas of the site contain concentrations of pig bones?' are bivariate archaeological questions that can be answered by such patterning within the data. Similar questions have been answered for many years without the aid of computers, but this new technology is virtually essential to analyse the large amounts of data from many modern excavations.

It is important here to consider the overall approach towards a large data-set that should be implicit in using computers as tools for statistical techniques. The key is to start with the simple and gradually to increase the complexity of the analysis by introducing more variables and, therefore, more sophisticated archaeological questions. This is an approach which is recommended generally throughout the social sciences and the resulting increased rigour is part of archaeology's attempt to become 'scientific'. As an example of this approach we can quickly look at some of the 150,000 pieces of animal bone from the Danebury excavations (Cunliffe, 1984). The first stage of analysis is to establish univariate distributions using histograms to answer questions like 'Do the mean, minimum and maximum number of bones per pit differ for pig, sheep and cattle?'. Bivariate distributions then introduce a second variable (phase, site position or pit type, perhaps) producing answers to more complex questions such as 'Does the number of pig bones increase with time?' or 'Are there more cattle bones in beehive pits than in cylindrical pits?'. It is here that one of many standard statistical tests could be used, depending on the type of data and question being asked. Here we will illustrate only one, the chi-squared test, which is one of the most popular tests of association in archaeology. This will demonstrate the methodology behind much inferential statistical work and show the importance of statistical significance rather than the more subjective archaeological significance.

Figure 19 shows a 'contingency table' for two variables: the three categories of site phase (early, middle and late) and two categories (present, absent) of sheep bones. The figures give the number of pits which either do or do not contain any sheep bones for each of the three phases. In the left-hand pair of columns the upper number in each cell is the actual number of pits in that category whereas the number in parenthesis is the expected number of pits (expected by the statistical theory which is explained below). The numbers in the pair of right-hand columns are the differences between expected and actual numbers in pits. It can be seen that in the early phase many fewer pits than expected (-31) do not contain sheep bones whereas in the late phase 26 'too many' do not contain them.

Statistical tests can be used to investigate how probable these observed figures are, if in truth there is no trend or pattern within them. What is being tested for, therefore, is how likely it is that the observed figures occurred randomly. This is the probability

Computer Archaeology

	P	A	P	A
E	95 (63)	428 (459)	+32	-31
M	11 (17)	131 (124)	-6	+7
L	6 (30)	249 (223)	-24	+26

X^2=43·2   p<0·1%

19. A contingency table for the presence/absence data of sheep bones in pits at Danebury hillfort for the early, middle and late site phases (E = early, M = middle, L = late, P = presence, A = absence, X^2 = chi-squared statistic, p = probability). (Source: Gary Lock.)

(p) in figure 19, which shows a greater statistical significance as it decreases in value. For example, p <0.1 means the results have a less than one in a thousand probability of happening by chance. From this we can conclude strong evidence for a relationship, or trend, within the figures. A common way of calculating p is to use the chi-squared statistic. As the difference between the expected and the observed increases, so does the chi-squared value, whilst p decreases correspondingly. The differences in figure 19 are statistically significant. This simple example has been used to answer a correspondingly simple archaeological question, 'Does the number of pits containing sheep bones change with time?' the answer being 'yes'. It is probable that during analysis more specific questions will arise of a much more complex nature. This complexity could be due to the number of variables involved, and it may be that one of the many multivariate statistical procedures could be of some help. As the name suggests, these manipulate cases (whether these be pottery sherds or pits) according to the values of many variables per case. Because of the huge number of calculations performed a mainframe computer is usually necessary, and great care must be taken to ensure that the results mean something archaeologically.

The area of multivariate techniques in which most progress has been made is numerical taxonomy and the associated classification methods, namely various forms of cluster analysis, principal components analysis, factor analysis, constellation analysis and multidimensional scaling. Each of these methods is described below with archaeological examples. The chapter concludes with the important methods of matrix analysis, seriation and spatial analysis, all of which have many archaeological applications.

Numerical taxonomy

Numerical taxonomy as applied to archaeology concerns the attachment of numerical quantities to certain attributes of archaeological materials, so that the description of the materials is represented purely by measurements. By calculating suitable similarity coefficients between pairs of objects based on these numerical quantities a classification may be constructed which is objectively calculated. The subjective judgement of the archaeologist will always have a place, however, in the initial choice of the variables to be used and in the interpretation of the results. Numerical taxonomy has applications in diverse fields, with about one thousand publications appearing annually, although the general philosophy was laid down by just a few workers, notably Sneath and Sokal (1973).

A distinction must be made between 'classification' and 'dissection'. A class or cluster must be internally cohesive and

20. A dendrogram showing the similarity of British beaker types based on profile and height. Clarke's intrusive groups AOC, W/MR, E, N/MR, N1/D, BW and N/NR are clearly separated into different branches on the dendrogram, and another possible intrusive group N2/N2(L) is separated. (Software: John Wilcock; data derived from David Clarke, 1970.)

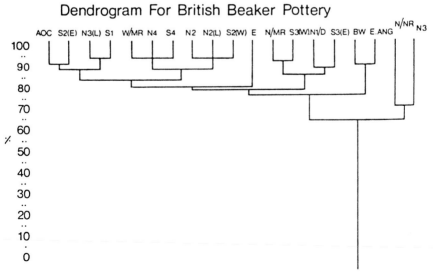

Dendrogram For British Beaker Pottery

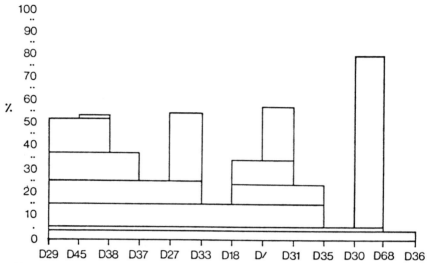

21. A skyline plot showing the similarity of common Samian pottery types based on profile and height. The 'skyscraper blocks' show different groups and the depth of the 'chasms' between the blocks is a measure of the isolation of the groups from each other. (Software: John Wilcock.)

isolated from the outside world by real and identifiable boundaries; herein lies a danger, for computer classification methods will always dissect the data into groups, whether or not clusters really exist in the sense of being meaningful archaeologically. Clusters may be required to be disjointed, or they may overlap (in which case they are also called clumps). Procedures usually lead to a hierarchy of clusters, which may be expressed in a tree-like form called a dendrogram (figure 20) or its equivalent, the skyline plot (figure 21).

The percentage levels at which these clusters form are called phenons. Figure 20 shows all the cases (types of pot) starting as separate entities and gradually clustering together to form just one cluster at the 65 per cent phenon level. Figure 21 represents clusters as 'skyscraper' blocks, hence the name 'skyline plot', the blocks gradually amalgamating as the clusters grow, and the depths of the chasms between the blocks showing how dissimilar are the clusters. Final amalgamation does not take place in this example until the 4 per cent phenon.

The process of classification may be regarded mathematically as the division of a large 'space' which includes all the units under

consideration, and which has dimensions corresponding to the attributes under study. A classification which is to be useful from an archaeological viewpoint should be:
(a) exhaustive, that is, each unit should belong to a class;
(b) exclusive, that is, no unit should belong to more than one class;
(c) unambiguously defined, that is, it should be possible to allocate each unit to a class without hesitation;
(d) natural, that is, units which appear to be 'alike' subjectively should belong to the same class.
A classification may be constructed either by defining the frontiers between the classes — this technique satisfies (a), (b) and (c) above but may fail criterion (d) — or by defining the core members of the classes and specifying that a new member must be more like the core of the class it is joining than other cores — this satisfies (a), (b) and (d) but may fail (c) because for 'hybrid' units it may not be immediately obvious to which class they belong.

Many different techniques devoted to forming such classifications exist as software within packages, and these techniques are collectively known as cluster analysis.

Cluster analysis

Clustering techniques employed on the computer are of several types. In the single-link (nearest-neighbour) strategy a search is made at each level of the hierarchy for the pair of units which are 'closest' according to the distance measure in use, and a fusion is made between them. But unfortunately the method has notorious 'chaining' properties, that is, quite diverse clusters eventually become joined by a series of nearest-neighbour links extended across the space between them. It therefore does not produce meaningful clusters for archaeological purposes.

The grouping can be improved from an archaeological point of view if a double-link or multiple-link strategy is used. Here a unit is allowed to join an existing cluster only if it is sufficiently close to two or more units already in the cluster. The idea may be extended to complete-linkage (furthest-neighbour) clustering, where a unit is allowed to join an existing cluster only if its similarities to all the cluster members (including the most distant) treated individually reached the required value. In general these methods have not found favour with archaeologists.

Most important for archaeology is the average-link strategy, where a unit joins an existing cluster if it is close enough to the mean properties of the cluster. There are undoubted mathematical objections to this procedure, but the archaeological results are generally most satisfactory.

These procedures have the disadvantage that once a unit is allocated to a cluster it can never escape from it. Although the unit was allocated to the most suitable cluster at the time of joining, this may have been early in the analysis. The unit is trapped in what might eventually be an unsuitable cluster, the cluster mean properties having so changed that the unit is finally closer to some other cluster mean than to its own cluster mean. This disadvantage is overcome in the k-means procedures, where units are allowed to migrate to the most suitable clusters at each stage (Hodson, 1971). The k-means procedures are attractive for archaeologists, yielding relatively homogeneous clusters with fewer anomalous units. Hodson is one of the few British archaeologists to have learnt about computing and to have developed classification procedures with archaeology primarily in mind; his most famous work was on data from the La Tène cemetery at Münsingen-Rain which yielded a large number of fibulae (brooches) of the pre-Roman iron age. Hodson also compared the objective computer classifications of the Münsingen-Rain brooches with several other archaeologists' 'intuitive' (subjective) classifications of the same data, with the amusing result that not only did the computer classification not agree with the archaeologists' classifications, but the archaeologists disagreed among themselves.

Many other workers have used cluster analysis on archaeological problems. Examples of assemblages analysed are European palaeolithic 'leafpoints' (Allsworth-Jones and Wilcock, 1974), Armorico-British daggers (Ottaway, 1974) and neolithic axes (Celoria and Wilcock, 1975).

Principal components analysis

The principal components method starts by representing each unit as a point in multidimensional space, which is defined by a set of axes mutually at right angles (orthogonal), each representing an attribute. The position of a point in space will depend on the respective values of the attributes of the corresponding unit. The aim of principal components analysis is to find a new set of orthogonal axes, which have the desirable property that the first new axis lies along the direction of maximum spread of the point distribution, the second lies along the direction of maximum residual spread, the third and subsequent axes account for the remaining spread, and there will be as many new axes as there

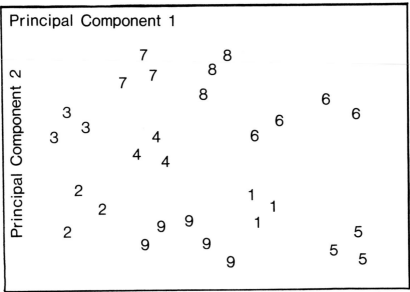

22. A typical principal components plot using the first two components for an assemblage of central German bell beakers. Each beaker is identified by the number of the cluster to which it was assigned by average link cluster analysis. It can be seen that the clusters occupy well defined areas, and this means that the two methods have given broadly similar results. The first two components accounted for over 92 per cent of the total variance in shape in this case and were identified as maximum width/height ratio (accounting for 82 per cent of the variance) and base width/maximum width ratio (10 per cent). (Copyright: *Science and Archaeology*; data compiled by Steve Shennan from records by Dr H. Behrens, Halle Landesmuseum.)

were old. The new set of axes are called components. Often for archaeological data the units can be adequately represented in the space defined by the first few components. This is a simplification of the actual distribution, with some distortion, but often the first two or three components can account for over 90 per cent of the total variance. For example, figure 22 shows a principal components plot for the first two components of an assemblage of central German bell beakers.

In this case two components were sufficient to account for 92 per cent of the total variance in shape, and thus the distribution could be represented in a two-dimensional scatterplot; the two components were deduced by the archaeologist user to be the maximum width/height ratio and the base width/maximum width ratio of the pots.

Alvey and Laxton (1974) have applied principal components to the forms of clay pipes, Ryan (1981) to the classification of Roman sites based on coin loss statistics, and Richards (1982) to Anglo-Saxon pot shapes.

Factor analysis

Factor analysis begins with the basic assumption that the overall description of an artefact or other archaeological entity is made up of varying proportions of factors which occur in all the entities under consideration, plus a specific part which is unique to each entity. The aim of the method is to discover the factors concerned in the description of all items. However, whereas principal components analysis always yields a unique fixed result for any given body of data, several different factor analyses are possible, which might well engender a feeling of unease in the archaeologist. Archaeologists have used it as a sort of cluster analysis, and the claimed results should be viewed with caution.

Constellation analysis

It is possible to divide the attributes of assemblages into different sets of constellations, for example a palaeolithic tool assemblage may have constellations referring to burin types, blade types, scraper types, and so on. When the similarities of assemblages are assessed, different results will be obtained if just the burin types are considered, or just the blade types, and so on; and if the assemblages are represented as points in multi-dimensional space their distances apart will be different according to whether constellation A or constellation B of the attributes is being studied. The two configurations in space may be fitted together as far as possible by scaling, reflection and rotation of axes, but in general there will not be an exact fit; the discrepancies may be expressed by a measure of misfit, being the sum of the square distances between corresponding points in the two configurations. Using this idea, Azoury and Hodson (1973) were able to formulate a method called constellation analysis. It has very wide applications in archaeology.

Multidimensional scaling

In the discussion on principal components analysis the idea of a spatial distribution of points representing units was explored. For principal components the axes of the distribution correspond to the first few components which account for most of the variance, and the number of dimensions is equal to the number of such components selected. In non-metric multidimensional scaling the idea is extended to a very large number of dimensions and the representation is in hyper-space unless the dimensions may be reduced to three or two, when diagrams interpretable by human observers may be generated. The method arranges points representing archaeological units in multi-dimensional space so that similar units are positioned close together and dissimilar units far apart. This presupposes that some measure of similarity (or dissimilarity) exists and that values called similarity (or dissimilarity) coefficients may be calculated for all pairs of units. The method is non-metric, that is, it takes no account of the absolute values of the coefficients, but considers only their relative values, sorting the coefficients into rank order of similarity (or dissimilarity). The points are then repositioned in space so that the inter-point distances, when ranked in order, yield as far as possible the same sequence of pairs of points as is given by the ranked dissimilarities (this is called a monotonic ascending sequence). The fit between the distances and dissimilarities will not in general be perfect; a goodness-of-fit measure called the stress may be calculated, which represents just how much the configuration (viewed as a structure of 'scaffolding poles') is in tension. The stress is minimised in the final configuration. The method requires a great many tedious calculations and is ideally suited to computer usage. The computer also attempts to minimise the number of dimensions, subject to the stress remaining low. Each reduction by one dimension is equivalent to 'squashing' the structure of 'scaffolding poles' connecting the points, and the stress will generally increase. The computer may be instructed to stop when the stress becomes too large and to print out the coordinates of all the points in the remaining dimensions. Luckily most archaeological distributions seem to fit into three or even two dimensions with little stress; this may be because there really are that number of dimensions inherent to the data, two of which may be geographical latitude and longitude (or northings, eastings) and one of which may be time. The final result may be plotted in perspective for three dimensions, or directly for two dimensions.

Figure 23 shows a two-dimensional scalogram for common forms of Samian pottery. Note that although multidimensional scaling does not start out as a clustering method, clusters are clearly visible: the group of large bowls Drag. 37, 29, 38 and 45 appears in the centre of the scalogram, while at the top is a group of flat platters and drinking cups, and at the bottom are some 'tall' pots. Various aids to interpretation of the structure of the data may be used. Figure 24 has the minimum spanning tree added, a method of showing the structure of the data and the most similar items. It is interesting to see how this is derived.

Consider the following matrix of the percentage similarities

Multidimensional Scaling Plot for

common Samian Ware forms

·35

36·

18/31

33 i8

27 31

38

29

37· 45

30

68

23. A scalogram (multidimensional scaling plot), shown in two dimensions, for some common Samian pottery forms. In the upper part of the diagram are a group of shallow bowls (Drag. 35, 36), platters (18, 18/31, 31) and drinking cups (33, 27). In the centre are deep bowls (37, 29, 45, 38) and at the bottom are some 'tall' pots (30, 68). Note that the evolutionary sequence (18 — 18/31 — 31) is correctly shown. (Copyright: *Science and Archaeology*.)

between the five objects A to E (thus B is 83 per cent similar to A, D is 25 per cent similar to E and so on):

	A	B	C	D	E
A	100	83	82	96	43
B	83	100	80	74	16
C	82	80	100	76	53
D	96	74	76	100	25
E	43	16	53	25	100

Using the similarity coefficient for a given pair of units only once, and ignoring the central diagonal (where objects are compared with themselves), we produce sorted list coefficients as follows:

A - D	96		B - D	74
A - B	83		C - E	53
A - C	82		A - E	43
B - C	80		D - E	25
C - D	76		B - E	16

The first link accepted is the highest coefficient A - D, so A and D are put in the output list. Thereafter the sorted list is scanned for the next highest link with a single unit in the output list, but not two such units in the list. Thus the next link selected is A - B (A is in the output list, but not B): then A - C (A in the list, not C); B -

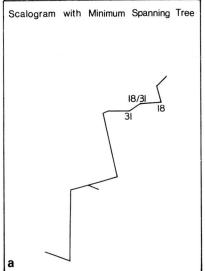

Scalogram with Minimum Spanning Tree

18/31
31   18

a

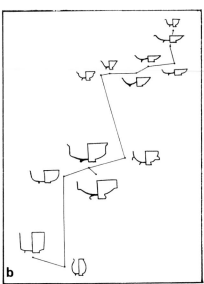

b

24. Different methods of portraying a scalogram with a minimum spanning tree: **(a)** shows the same common Samian ware forms illustrated in figure 23, with a minimum spanning tree added to show the structure of the data, each pot being joined to the other pot to which it is most similar. Note that the evolutionary sequence Drag. 18 — 18/31 — 31 is indicated. **(b)** is the same with pottery profiles added. **(c)** shows a minimum spanning tree for British beaker pottery, with Clarke's 'instrusive groups' indicated by heavy arrows — a further intrusive group may be indicated by the sharp bend at N2/N2(L), and N3 may be another; compare with figure 20. (Software: John Wilcock; copyright: *Science and Archaeology*; beaker pottery data derived from David Clarke, 1970.)

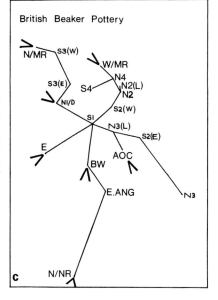

British Beaker Pottery

N/MR S3(W)
S3(E) S4   W/MR
NI/D   N4
              N2(L)
              N2
S1   S2(W)
      N3(L)
              S2(E)
E   AOC
  BW
  E.ANG   N3
c   N/NR

C, C - D and B - D are ignored because both units are in the list; and C - E is finally taken. The *algorithm* scans from the head of the sorted list each time, ignoring links already selected and those with two units in the output list, and continues to scan until all units are linked.

The minimum spanning tree generated is thus:

$$D - A - B$$
$$|$$
$$C$$
$$|$$
$$E$$

For large assemblages it may be necessary to cluster the units and use group mean properties for multidimensional scaling input; if this is done it is helpful if the relative importance of the groups is known, and this may be indicated by arbitrary circles of area proportional to the number of units in a cluster (see figure 25). Finally 'contour' lines may be added to illustrate the formation of clusters on a scalogram. The phenon levels may be derived from a dendrogram of the same data, and the result is called a Wroclaw diagram (see figure 26).

Flinders Petrie and matrix analysis

It is possible to store qualitative presence/absence data referring to archaeological artefacts, features or assemblages in a rectangular representation called an incidence matrix. The matrix is made up of elements, which in the case of presence/absence data may be the number 1 (for presence) or the number 0 (for absence); each element lies in a row of the matrix which represents the description of an item, and in a column of the matrix which represents the presence or absence of a given attribute. Thus each row describes one artefact, feature or

25. A scalogram with arbitrary circles of area proportional to the number of arte-facts in a group; in the multi-dimensional scaling run, in order to reduce the data, large groups were treated as single en-tities with parameters corresponding to the group centroids. (Data provided by Michael Walker.)

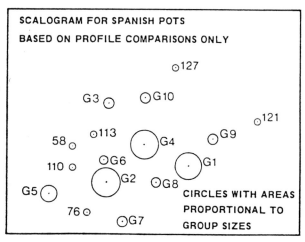

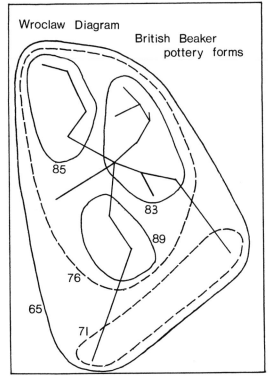

Wroclaw Diagram

British Beaker
pottery forms

85
83
89
76
65
71

26. A Wroclaw diagram for the British beaker pottery illustrated in figure 24 (c). This is a scalogram with minimum spanning tree, with groups derived by a cluster analysis program also added. Each group is indicated by a closed curve, and the percentage similarity phenon levels at which these groups form (see the dendrogram of figure 20) are also shown. (Copyright: *Science and Archaeology;* beaker pottery data derived from David Clarke, 1970.)

assemblage in terms of the presence or absence of specific attributes.

The first archaeologist to make use of any statistical method was Sir W. M. Flinders Petrie. He was working on pottery types found in Egyptian neolithic graves and effectively constructed and analysed a matrix by manual methods. Petrie examined nine hundred Predynastic graves containing about eight hundred types of pottery and recorded the contents of each grave on a slip of paper, later sorting them according to common types of pottery. These slips of paper have now been lost, but the incidence matrix would have had nine hundred rows (representing the graves) and eight hundred columns (representing the pottery types).

Once the incidence matrix exists it may be operated upon by manipulative methods. The first step is to generate a new symmetric matrix (with an equal number of rows and columns) from the incidence matrix; two such matrices exist, one formed by counting the number of times each attribute occurs in conjunction with every other in turn (the R technique), and the second by counting the number of common attribute states between all pairs of artefacts (the Q technique). Thus an incidence matrix for one hundred artefacts described by twenty properties, for example, will yield a twenty by twenty attribute-attribute R square matrix which compares the properties and a one hundred by one hundred artefact-artefact Q square matrix which compares the artefacts. The new matrix is now examined to see where the highest counts occur. Down the top left to bottom right diagonal (where each attribute occurrence pattern or each artefact is compared with itself) the counts will all be maximum (equal to the number of artefacts or number of attributes respectively). It seems reasonable that the 'essence' of the matrix could be determined if all high counts were to occur near this central diagonal as far as possible, and this may be achieved by reordering columns and rows. The method is highly important for the seriation technique (see below) applied to the artefact-artefact (or assemblage-assemblage) comparison square matrix, but it is of less obvious validity for manipulation of the attribute-attribute matrix.

Kendall (1971) explored the matrix ordering methods and their frontiers with seriation and multidimensional scaling in great detail. He developed the Kendall-Petrie Concentration Principle, stated for Petrie's collection of graves as 'If the typology is chronologically significant, and when the graves have been correctly ordered (or anti-ordered), then the sequence date ranges for the individual types will be found to have been individually or in some communal way minimised'. He referred to the reordering of rows and columns of a square matrix to bunch the high counts together near the central diagonal as 'Petrifaction' and showed that this was of direct value in seriation.

Seriation

Seriation is allied to matrix analysis in the sense that if a reordered matrix exhibits a one-dimensional trend the single dimension may be time and the order of the rows of the matrix may then by implication indicate the chronological ordering of the assemblages. Note that a linear development is assumed, and branched chains of development are not considered: the method forces the data into a linear sequence whether they fit or not.

The essential theory behind the seriation method was first developed by Brainerd and Robinson (Robinson, 1951). The Brainerd-Robinson partnership was a classic example of the cooperation of an archaeologist and a mathematician to produce a method which neither could have produced alone.

Consider the following assemblages of artefacts:

	iron tools	beaker pottery	stone tools	Samian ware	bronze tools		Row weights
A	1			1	1		1
B			1				2
C		1			1	incidence	3
D	1					matrix	4
E	1				1		5
F		1	1				6
column sums	10	9	8	1	9		
column averages	3.33	4.5	4	1	3		

In the incidence matrix above, the rows represent six site assemblages and the columns typical artefacts. The occurrence of a number 1 indicates that the particular type of artefact is found on the given site. This matrix is unordered and the 1s are widely scattered; the aim is to get the 1s as close to the central diagonal as possible by reordering the columns and rows, when both the artefact types and the sites will hopefully be seriated. Let us commence by giving the first row a weight of 1, the second row a weight of 2 and so on. The average weight of the 1 entries in each column is now calculated. Thus for the first column the average weight is $(1 + 4 + 5)/3 = 3.33$, for the second column it is $(3 + 6)/2 = 4.5$ and for the others 4, 1 and 3. Columns are now reordered according to their weight:

	SW	BT	IT	ST	BP	row sums	row averages
A	1	1	1			6	2
B				1		4	4
C		1			1	7	3.5
D			1			3	3
E		1	1			5	2.5
F				1	1	9	4.5
column weights	1	2	3	4	5		

Row weights are now calculated. These are 2, 4, 3.5, 3, 2.5 and 4.5. The rows are now reordered according to their weight:

	SW	BT	IT	ST	BP	Row weights
A	1	1	1			1
E		1	1			2
D			1			3
C		1			1	4
B				1		5
F				1	1	6
column sums	1	7	6	11	10	
column averages	1	2.33	2	5.5	5	Reorder columns

	SW	IT	BT	BP	ST	row sums	row averages
A	1	1	1			6	2
E		1	1			5	2.5
D			1			2	2
C			1	1		7	3.5
B					1	5	5
F				1	1	9	4.5
column weights	1	2	3	4	5	Reorder rows	

	SW	IT	BT	BP	ST	row weights
A	1	1	1			1
D		1				2
E		1	1			3
C			1	1		4
F				1	1	5
B					1	6
column sums	1	6	8	9	11	
column averages	1	2	2.67	4.5	5.5	

Column averages are now already in the correct order so the procedure halts and the matrix has been seriated as far as is possible. Using further archaeological knowledge or perhaps radiocarbon dating in conjunction with this seriation, it is predicted that B is the earliest site (stone tools only) and A the latest site (Samian ware and Roman iron and bronze tools), and also that the age order of the artefact types is stone tools, beaker pottery, bronze tools, iron tools and Samian ware. A particularly simple example has been chosen, and the correct order of the columns is common sense to an archaeologist faced with the given artefacts, but it serves to illustrate the principle of the method and in most examples the order of the columns and hence the chronological ordering of the artefacts is what the archaeologist is hoping to achieve by the method. However, the method is not guaranteed to succeed.

Some archaeologists have also attempted seriation of the derived artefact-artefact and site-site square matrices, but the validity of this procedure is more dubious.

Spatial analysis

There is a whole group of statistical techniques devoted to spatial analysis. Most of these are derived from other disciplines, mainly geography and ecology, and include methods such as nearest-neighbour analysis and trend surface analysis. They are all adequately described, with examples, in Hodder and Orton (1976).

7
Conclusions

Are these applications of the computer in archaeology all worthwhile? And is the computer here to stay in archaeology? The answer to both these questions must decidely be yes. The previous chapters have dealt with the capture and retrieval of data, statistics and graphics. These steps form a logical sequence and we can envisage them in archaeological computer systems of the future forming an integrated whole with *menu* selection, a strategy first attempted in the PLUTARCH software in 1970 (Wilcock, 1974). The final stage will be automated publication, easily satisfied by the integration of graphics plus a 'word-processing' package, of which many are already available. Another future advance is in the use of computer *networks* so that archaeologists based at workstations many miles apart will be able to communicate.

There are two problems standing in the way of this computer-ised future which are not to do with machines but to do with archaeologists themselves. The first is the rather conservative attitude of the traditionally humanities-trained archaeologist when it comes to understanding anything 'scientific'.

This has often been solved by 'hunting in pairs', with an archaeologist and a computer scientist working together, each with sympathy for the problems and working practices of the other's discipline. Moreover, some courses in archaeology include training in the use of computer packages, and it seems that most young archaeologists appreciate that the computer has indeed something to offer. There is still a long way to go, however, until every undergraduate course in archaeology includes a basic grounding in computing and statistics.

The second problem is archaeologists' inability to agree on any form of standardisation. This is the cause of much debate within archaeology and seems unlikely to be resolved quickly. Standard-isation is theoretically possible at two levels. The first is in the use of compatible hardware and software, which is essential if any sort of large-scale communication is to happen. The second possible level of standardisation is in the coding and structure of data. This is a philosophically difficult line to enforce because it would stifle freedom of thought and lead to academic stagnation. Who is to say which pottery classification is 'correct' and the one to be used? This debate predates computers (although they have somewhat forced the issue) as specialists have always disagreed. It is to be hoped that they always will, as this is a sure sign that there is life after the computer.

8
Bibliography

Periodicals

Computer archaeology is a respectable international discipline in its own right, with frequent conferences, seminars and publications. Among the most useful periodicals are:

Archaeological Computing Newsletter (Britain), 1984 onwards. A quarterly newsletter written by and for archaeologists whatever their level of computer expertise. Available from: Department of Computing, North Staffordshire Polytechnic, Blackheath Lane, Stafford ST18 0AD.

Computer Applications in Archaeology (Britain), 1973 onwards. Publication of the papers presented at annual conferences held at several university venues over the years.

Computers and the Humanities (USA), 1967 onwards.

Journal of Archaeological Science (Britain), 1974 onwards.

Newsletter of Computer Archaeology (USA), 1965-79, renamed *Advances in Computer Archaeology* in 1983. Editors S. W. Gaines and W. K. Wait, with an international board of associate editors.

Science and Archaeology (Britain), 1970 onwards. Editor J. D. Wilcock.

World Archaeology, occasional issues from 1969 onwards, particularly volume 1, number 3 (1970) and volume 14, number 1 (1982) on quantitative methods.

Books and papers

Probably the best overall introduction to computers in archaeology is provided by Richards and Ryan (1985). Doran and Hodson (1975) cover some of the same ground but in much more detail. In general, however, they are more concerned with statistical areas, as are Orton (1982) and Hodder and Orton (1976). Two books contain 'state-of-the-art' papers describing the whole range of computer applications in archaeology; these are Martlew (1984) and Cooper and Richards (1985).

Allsworth-Jones, P., and Wilcock, J. D., 1974. 'A computer-assisted study of European palaeolithic "leafpoints": methodology and preliminary results', *Science and Archaeology*, volume 11 25-46.

Alvey, R. C., and Laxton, R. R., 1974. 'Analysis of some Nottingham clay pipes', *Science and Archaeology*, volume 13 3-12.

Angell, I. O., 1981. *A Practical Introduction to Computer Graphics*. Macmillan Press.

Azoury, I., and Hodson, F. R., 1973. 'Comparing palaeolithic assemblages: Ksar Akil, a case study', *World Archaeology*, volume 4, number 3 292-306.

Baillie, M. G. L., 1982. *Tree-ring Dating and Archaeology* (pages 79-92). Croom Helm.

Booth, B., Brough, R., and Pryor, F., 1984. 'The flexible storage of site data: a microcomputer application', *Journal of Archaeological Science*, volume 11 81-9.

Callow, P., 1976. 'British and French handaxe series' in *Computer Applications in Archaeology*, editor S. Laflin, 33-40.

Celoria, F. S. C., and Wilcock, J. D., 1975. 'A computer-assisted classification of British neolithic axes and a comparison with some Mexican and Guatemalan axes', *Science and Archaeology*, volume 16 11-29.

Chenhall, R. G., 1967a. 'Museum cataloguing by computer', *Computers and the Humanities*, volume 1 240.

Chenhall, R. G., 1976b. 'The description of archaeological data in computer language', *American Antiquity*, volume 32 161-7.

Clarke, D. L., 1968. *Analytical Archaeology*. Methuen and Company.

Clarke, D. L., 1970. *Beaker Pottery of Great Britain and Ireland*. Cambridge University Press.

Cooper, M. A., and Richards, J. D. (editors), 1985. *Current Issues in Archaeological Computing*. BAR International Series volume 271, Oxford.

Cowgill, G., 1973. 'Teotihuacan data bank', *Newsletter of Computer Archaeology*, volume 8, number 4 6.

Cunliffe, B. W., 1984. *Danebury. An iron age hillfort in Hampshire* (two volumes). CBA Research Report Number 52.

Doran, J. E., and Hodson, F. R., 1975. *Mathematics and Computers in Archaeology*. Edinburgh University Press.

Duncan, J. M., and Main, P. L., 1977. 'The drawing of archaeological sections and plans by computer', *Science and Archaeology*, volume 20 17-26.

Fletcher, M., and Lock, G. R., 1984. 'Post-built structures at Danebury hillfort. An analytical search method with statistical discussion', *Oxford Journal of Archaeology*, volume 3, number 2 175-96.

Graham, I. D. G., 1976. 'Intelligent terminals for excavation recording' in *Computer Applications in Archaeology*, editor S.Laflin, pages 48-52.

Hodder, I., and Orton, C., 1976. *Spatial Analysis in Archaeology*. Cambridge University Press.

Hodson, F. R., 1971. 'Numerical typology and prehistoric archaeology' in *Mathematics in the Archaeological and Historical Sciences* (pages 30-45), editors F. R. Hodson, D. G. Kendall and P. Tautu, Edinburgh University Press.

Kendall, D. G., 1971. 'Seriation from abundance matrices' in *Mathematics in the Archaeological and Historical Sciences* (pages 215-52), editors F. R. Hodson, D. G. Kendall, and P. Tautu, Edinburgh University Press.

Laflin, S., 1973. 'Computer system for county gazetteers', *Science and Archaeology*, volume 9 26-8.

Light, R. B., and Roberts, D. A. (editors), 1984. *Microcomputers in Museums*. MDA Occasional Paper 7, Museum Documentation Association.

Lock, G. R., 1980. 'Some archaeological uses of the PICASO computer graphics package', *Science and Archaeology*, volume 22 16-24.

Lock, G. R., 1983. 'Computer-assisted seriation of the pits at Danebury hillfort', *Science and Archaeology*, volume 25 3-8.

Lock, G. R., 1984. 'The computerization of the Danebury archive' in *Danebury: an Iron Age Hillfort in Hampshire*, B. W. Cunliffe, volume 1 8-9.

Lock, G. R., and Reilly, P., 1986. 'Crop-marks at Stramshall, near Uttoxeter, Staffordshire: an unknown Roman camp?' *Staffordshire Archaeological Studies*, new series 3 13-19.

Martlew, R. (editor), 1984. *Information Systems in Archaeology*. New Standard Archaeology, Alan Sutton Publishing.

McNett, C. W., Junior, 1981. 'Computer graphics in the analysis of archaeological data' in *Data Bank Applications in Archaeology* (pages 90-9), editor S. W. Gaines, University of Arizona Press.

Orton, C. R., 1982. *Mathematics in Archaeology*. Cambridge University Press.

Ottaway, B., 1974. 'Cluster analysis of impurity patterns in Armorico-British daggers', *Archaeometry*, volume 16 221-31.

Powlesland, D., 1983. 'Pots, pits and portables', *Practical Computing*, June 144-6.

Powlesland, D., 1985. *Archaeology and Computers*. CBA.

Richards, J. D., 1982. 'Anglo-Saxon pot shapes: cognitive

56   *Computer Archaeology*

investigations', *Science and Archaeology*, volume 24 33-46.
Richards, J. D., and Ryan, N. S., 1985. *Data processing in Archaeology*. Cambridge Manuals in Archaeology, Cambridge University Press.
Robinson, W. S., 1951. 'A method for chronologically ordering archaeological deposits', *American Antiquity*, volume 16, number 4 293-301.
Ryan, N. S., 1981. 'Microcomputer analysis of Romano-British coin loss' in *Computer Applications in Archaeology*, editor S. Laflin, 162-71.
Shennan, S. J., and Wilcock, J. D., 1975. 'Shape and style variation in central German bell beakers: a computer-assisted study', *Science and Archaeology*, volume 15 17-31.
Sneath, P. H. A., and Sokal, C. R., 1973. *Numerical Taxonomy: The Principles and Practice of Numerical Classification*. W. H. Freeman.
Spicer, R., 1985. 'Stereoscopic representation of archaeological data — a case for drawing conclusions in depth,' *Science and Archaeology*, volume 27 13-24.
Stewart, J. D. (editor), 1980. *Microcomputers in Archaeology*. MDA Occasional Paper 4, Museum Documentation Association.
Walker, M. J., 1981. 'Petroglyphs' in *Data Bank Applications in Archaeology*, pages 112-15, editor S. W. Gaines. University of Arizona Press.
Wilcock, J. D., 1969. 'Computers and Camelot: South Cadbury, an exercise in computer archaeology', *Spectrum, British Science News*, volume 60 7-9. Central Office of Information, HMSO, London.
Wilcock, J. D., 1974. 'The facilities of the PLUTARCH system', *Science and Archaeology*, volume 11 16-24.
Wilcock, J. D., 1975. 'Archaeological context sorting by computer' in *Computer Applications in Archaeology*, editor S. Laflin, 93-7.
Wilcock, J. D., 1978. 'The automated archaeologist' in *Computer Applications in Archaeology*, editor S. Laflin, 49-52.
Wilcock, J. D., 1981 (a). 'STRATA — the microcomputer version' in *Computer Applications in Archaeology*, editor I. Graham, 112-14.
Wilcock, J. D., 1981(b). 'Roman inscriptions and the use of the PLUTARCH system' in *Data Bank Applications in Archaeology*, pages 107-12, editor S. W. Gaines. University of Arizona Press.

Wilcock, J. D., 1983. 'Data processing' in *Guidelines for the Processing and Publication of Medieval Pottery from Excavations,* Directorate of Ancient Monuments and Historic Buildings Occasional Papers number 5, editors H. Blake and P. Davey, Department of the Environment, 23-34.

Wilcock, J. D., Otlet, R. L., and Walker, A. J., 1983. 'Proposals for a high-level international record structure for radio-carbon databases', *Symposium on Archaeometry Abstracts,* volume 23 122-3.

Young, C. J. (editor), 1980. *Guidelines for the Processing and Publication of Roman Pottery from Excavations,* Directorate of Ancient Monuments and Historic Buildings Occasional Papers number 4, Department of the Environment.

9
Glossary

This book has been written using as few technical terms as possible. Computing science has its own technical vocabulary, however, like all other sciences, and inevitably some of these 'jargon' words have had to be used in the text. The purely technical words coined for and unique to computing should cause little difficulty to the average archaeologist; all that is required here is a concise definition in simple terms. However, numerous 'plain English' words have been taken over and joined together into phrases which can be unintelligible to a non-specialist. Also, since much development in computing has taken place in the United States, American spellings of English words appear; these spellings, while they can be jarring to an English specialist, are 'sanctified' by common usage, and the computer scientist would regard any attempts to anglicise the spelling as pure pedantry. The use of acronyms is very prevalent: some are very cryptic, others are allegorical, witty or 'clever', and this can be an added source of irritation. Thousands of terms are in everyday use in computing, and no attempt has been made to cover these comprehensively. But it is hoped that these remarks and the definitions of selected terms given below in simple plain language will prove useful to the archaeologist attempting to break the barrier of computer terminology.

Access: the process of obtaining *data* from a *peripheral* device or the computer memory. Also used as a verb.

Algorithm: a series of instructions or procedural steps for the solution of a given problem.

Alphanumeric: a *character* set containing the letters of the alphabet and numerals.

ASCII: American Standard Code for Information Interchange.

Backing store: a form of computer long-term memory based on a peripheral device such as discs or tape.

Bit: a unit of storage equivalent to one binary digit, 0 or 1.

Boolean: a system of algebra named after its inventor, the mathematician George Boole (1815-64), based on the ideas of Aristotelian logic in which a variable may only be true or false; also applied to such a variable used in a computer *program*.

Byte: a unit of storage equivalent to eight *bits*.

Central processing unit (cpu): the part of a computer that contains the *memory* and performs mathematical and logical operations.

Character: one of a set of symbols used by a computer, for example letters of the alphabet, numerals and punctuation marks represented by a code such as *ASCII.*

Coding system: a standardised method of representing data in symbolic form.

Cursor: a flashing symbol indicating the next character entry position on a screen.

Data: group of characters or operands giving values operated upon by a computer program. Although normally plural in English (and treated as such in this book), in computing it is usually treated as a collective noun — 'data are' is thought to be pedantic. Treated as different to 'information', which is processed data.

Database: a *file* of *data* structured so that a general database management system may perform operations on it, but the operations do not apply any constraints on the file design or content. Different from a databank, which is a file of specific data.

Data capture: the collection of raw *data* for computer processing.

Data processing: a series of operations performed on *data.*

Data structure: the ordering and layout of *data* for specific computer operations.

Descriptive statistics: a set of statistical techniques used to condense data into an understandable form. Includes graphical methods, such as histograms and piecharts, and values such as mean and standard deviation.

Device: a mechanism to perform *storage, input* or *output.* See also *peripheral.*

Digitising table: a *device* for capturing graphical data. See also *tablet.*

Direct access: a method of file access allowing each *record* to be accessed with equal ease. Also called random access.

Disc drive: a *peripheral device* which drives a *magnetic disc.*

Dot matrix: dots arranged on a rectangular grid which may be used to form a character on a screen or *printer.*

Field: A subdivision of a *record* which contains one piece of information.

File: an organised collection of *records.*

Floppy disc: a flexible *magnetic disc* enclosed in an envelope with holes for motor pressure pad, read/write heads and sector addressing markers. Relatively cheap, and common on *micro-computers.*

Hard copy: *output* from a computer which is on paper, such as a printout or picture.

Hardware: the physical units making up a computer system.

High-level communication format: the information structure intended as a common intermediary between any two incompatible computer systems.

Indexed sequential file: a *file* which has a serial (sequential) data structure, such as a *magnetic tape,* organised in such a way that one part contains an index which serves to locate items in other parts of the file.

Inferential statistics: a group of statistical techniques which can be used for testing hypotheses.

Information retrieval: a process of categorisation and storage of information so that it may later be matched against a request for information satisfying specified criteria.

Input: a process of transferring *data* from a *peripheral* to the computer memory. Also used as a verb.

Input/output (I/O) devices: devices used to communicate with the computer *(input)* and to receive messages from the computer *(output).*

Inverted file: a form of file organisation which is 'item-on-term' that is, each characteristic term or *keyword* carries pointers to all items having that characteristic.

Keyboard: A *device* for encoding characters by pressing keys for *input* to the computer.

Keyword: a signficant word used in information retrieval; for example in a paper entitled 'A computer-assisted study of European palaeolithic leafpoints' keywords are 'Europe' (provenance), 'palaeolithic' (period) and 'leafpoint' (type of artefact), the remaining words having no significance, except possibly 'computer' (for those interested in computer archaeology).

Kilobyte (Kb): a unit of storage equal to 1,024 *bytes.*

Language: a set of coded instruction types, with well defined rules of combination, used to control a computer.

Line-printer: a *printer* which outputs one line of print at a time.

Logic: the science of formal reasoning; in computers applied to circuit design or to program structure using *Boolean* algebra.

Magnetic disc: a *storage device (backing store)* consisting of one or more flat circular discs coated with a magnetic medium; includes *floppy discs,* hard discs, *Winchester* discs.

Magnetic tape: a *storage device (backing store)* consisting of a strip of plastic material coated with a magnetic medium; includes cassette tapes, reels of tape.

Mainframe computer: originally the main metal frame of the arithmetic unit of a large computer. Used colloquially to refer to the largest type of computer.

Megabyte (Mb): a unit of storage equal to approximately 1,000,000 *bytes.*

Memory: the part of a computer in which *data* and *progams* are stored during execution.

Menu: the choice of software processes, displayed on and selected from a screen.

Microcomputer: a small computer designed for personal use. Usually cheap and with rudimentary *peripherals.*

Microprocessor: the *CPU* of a microcomputer, usually contained within one silicon chip.

Mini-computer: a small-scale *mainframe computer.*

Network: organised interfaces to link several computers, with communication of *software* and *data.*

Operating system: a set of programs, usually supplied with the computer, that provide communication between the user, *programs* and *hardware.*

Output: the process of transferring data from the computer memory to a peripheral. Also applied to the results of a computer program, and may additionally be used as a verb.

Package: a generalised program written for a major application in such a way that a user's particular *hardware* and *data* organisation will not make the operation any less useful, for example *database* management system, *word processor.*

Peripheral: a machine unit on the 'periphery' of the computer; an *input* or *output* device.

Plotter: a device which draws on paper to produce graphics *output.*

Printer: an *output* device which converts *data* into printed characters.

Program: (note the American spelling) a set of instructions written to solve a particular problem on the computer.

Random access: a storage organisation which allows any item to be located as quickly as any other, for example computer internal memory, or magnetic disc.

Record: a group of data representing one entity in a file.

Relational database: *database* organisation where items are linked by *relations,* for example one-to-one, one-to-many, many-to-one, many-to-many.

ROM (Read Only Memory): storage which holds permanent *data* that cannot be altered by program, for example operating system, BASIC interpreter, dot-matrix character layouts.

Sequential file: a storage organisation which places *records* in sequence. The records can only be *accessed* in the sequence in which they are stored. A common example of sequential access storage is magnetic tape.

Serial access: access to *records* in a data *file* in the order in which they occur in a given storage device.

Software: a term used in contrast to *hardware* to refer to all programs which can be used on a computer system. Software includes user programs, packages, assemblers, compilers, interpreters, utility programs, trace routines, test and diagnostic programs, operating systems, and so on.

Storage: a physical *device* used to remember data, or the process of recording data in such a device.

Tablet: a rectangular pad used to locate points in a graphics system using a stylus or crosswires. An alternative to a light pen.

Thesaurus: a full list of *keywords* allowed in an information retrieval system. Used to avoid synonyms and to validate keywords.

User-friendly: an adjective describing *software* which is easy to operate by a naive user, lacking cryptic messages, and so on.

Visual display unit (VDU): an *input/output device* with *keyboard* and a monitor screen combined in one unit.

Winchester disc: a small hard *magnetic disc* system often used on microcomputers.

Word processing: the manipulation of text by a computer in the preparation of printed documents.

Index

Page numbers in italic refer to illustrations on those pages.